Shaolin Days and DeKalb Nights

Victor Gastelum
&
Robert Vodicka

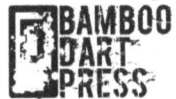

LOS ANGELES † NEW YORK † LONDON † MELBOURNE

Shaolin Days and DeKalb Nights by Victor Gastelum and Robert Vodicka

ISBN: 978-1-947240-49-0

eISBN: 978-1-947240-50-6

Copyright © 2022 Victor Gastelum and Robert Vodicka. All rights reserved.

First Printing 2022

Cover art by Victor Gastelum

Layout and design by Mark Givens

For information:

Bamboo Dart Press

chapbooks@bamboodartpress.com

Bamboo Dart Press 018

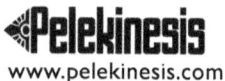
www.pelekinesis.com

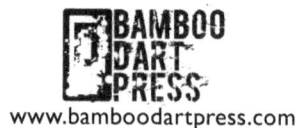
www.bamboodartpress.com

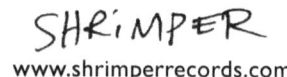
www.shrimperrecords.com

"To the being fully alive, the future is not ominous but a promise; it surrounds the present as a halo. It consists of possibilities that are felt as a possession of what is now and here. In life that is truly life, everything overlaps and merges. But all too often we exist in apprehensions of what the future may bring, and are divided within ourselves. Even when not overanxious, we do not enjoy the present because we subordinate it to that which is absent. Because of the frequency of this abandonment of the present to the past and future, the happy periods of an experience that is now complete because it absorbs itself into memories of the past and anticipations of the future, come to constitute an esthetic ideal. Only when the past ceases to trouble and anticipations of the future are not perturbing is a being wholly united with his (sic) environment and therefore fully alive. Art celebrates with peculiar intensity the moments in which the past reinforces the present and in which the future is a quickening of what is now."
    —John Dewey, *Art As Experience*, New York: Perigee Books, 1934), p. 18.

"It was a fine cry - loud and long - but it had no bottom and it had no top, just circles and circles of sorrow."
    —Toni Morrison, *Sula*, (New York: Knopf, 1974), p. 174.

Shaolin Days
&
DeKalb Nights

Peripheral Justice

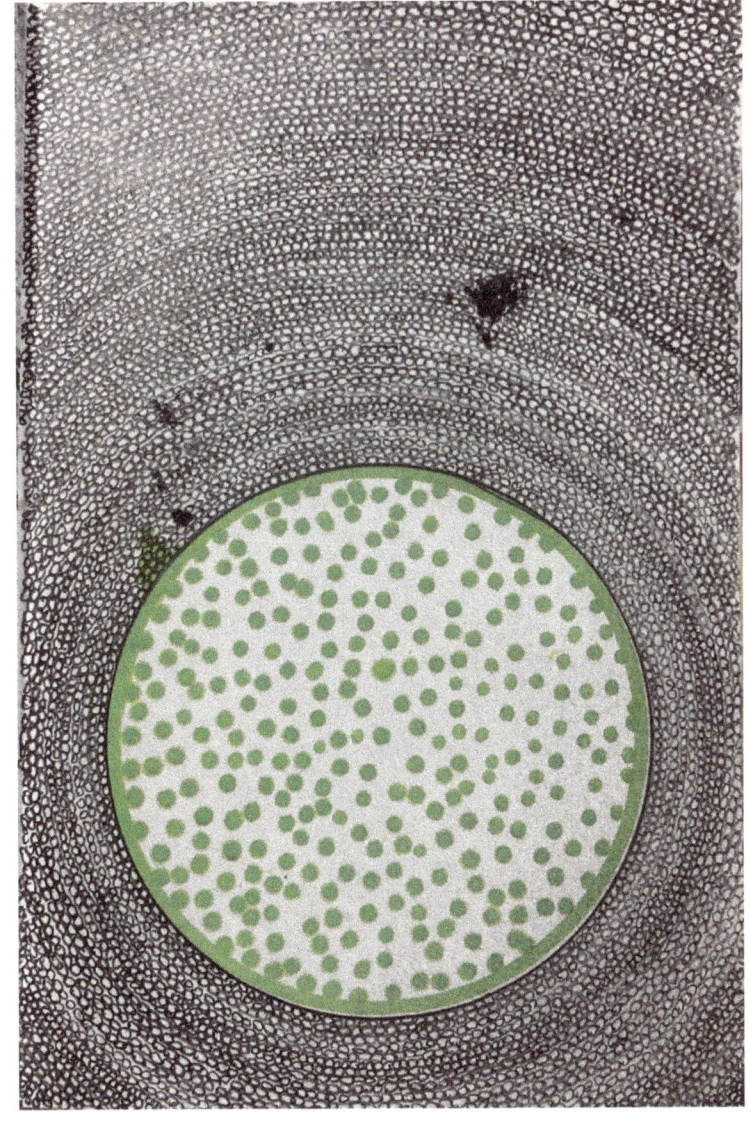

Heavy metal fatigue

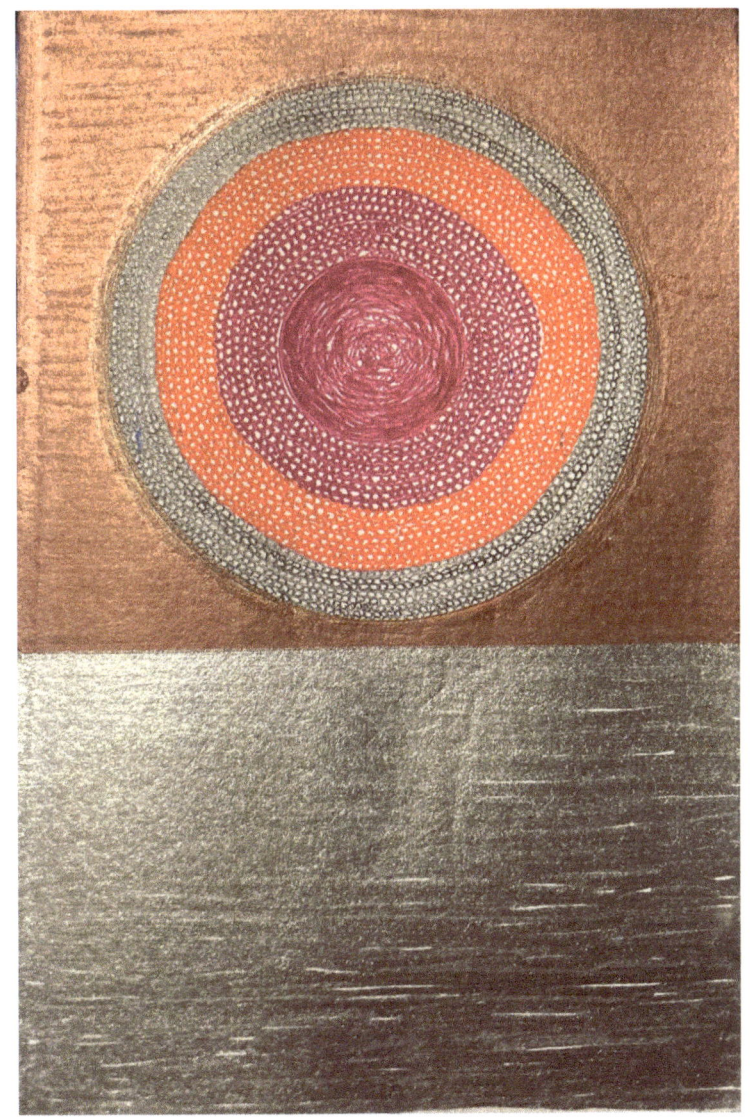

Favorite mother

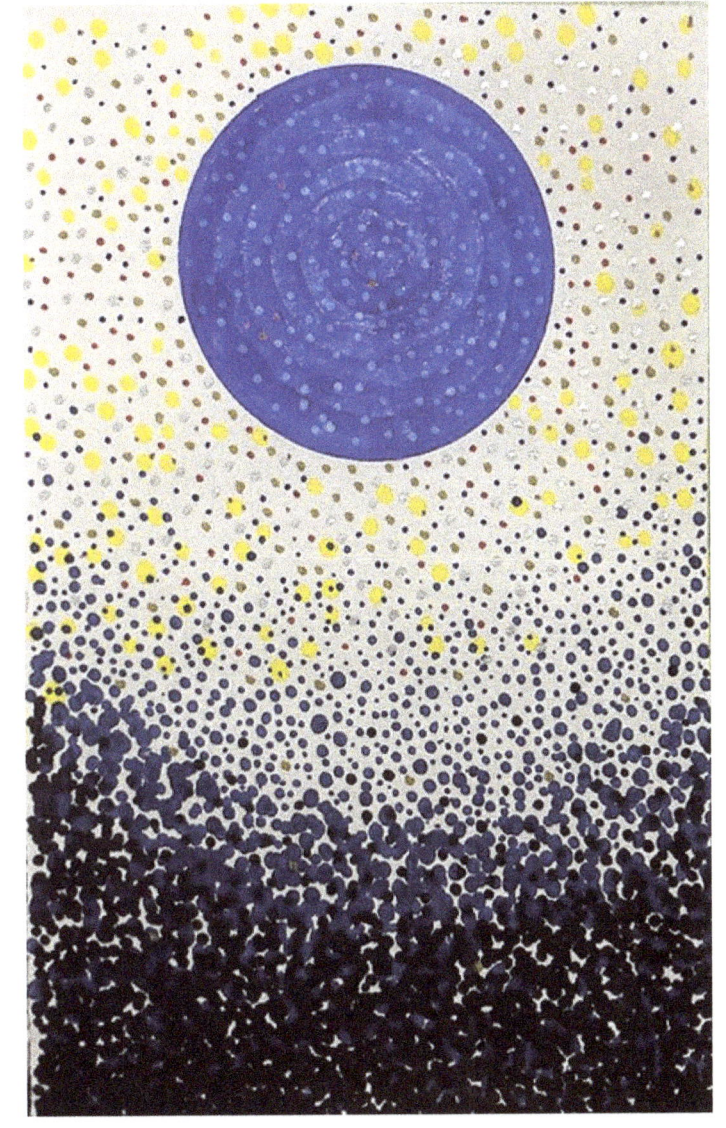

Trees of North Korea

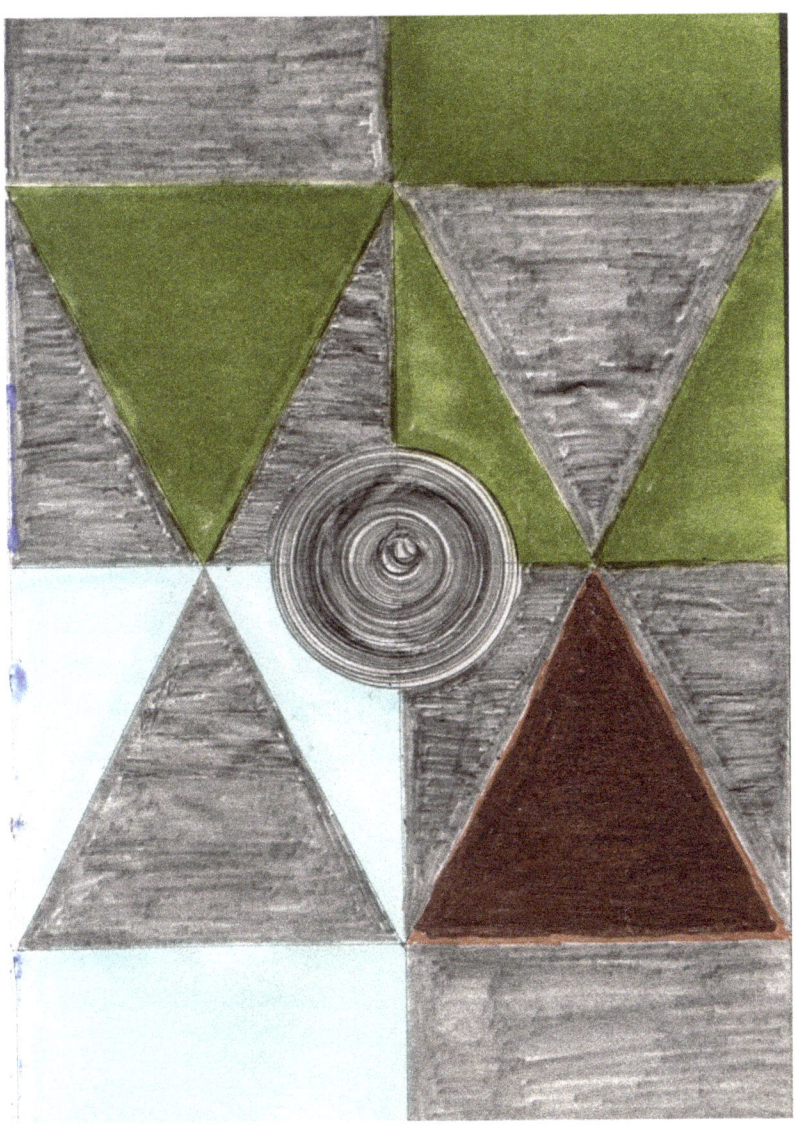

Solitary partner

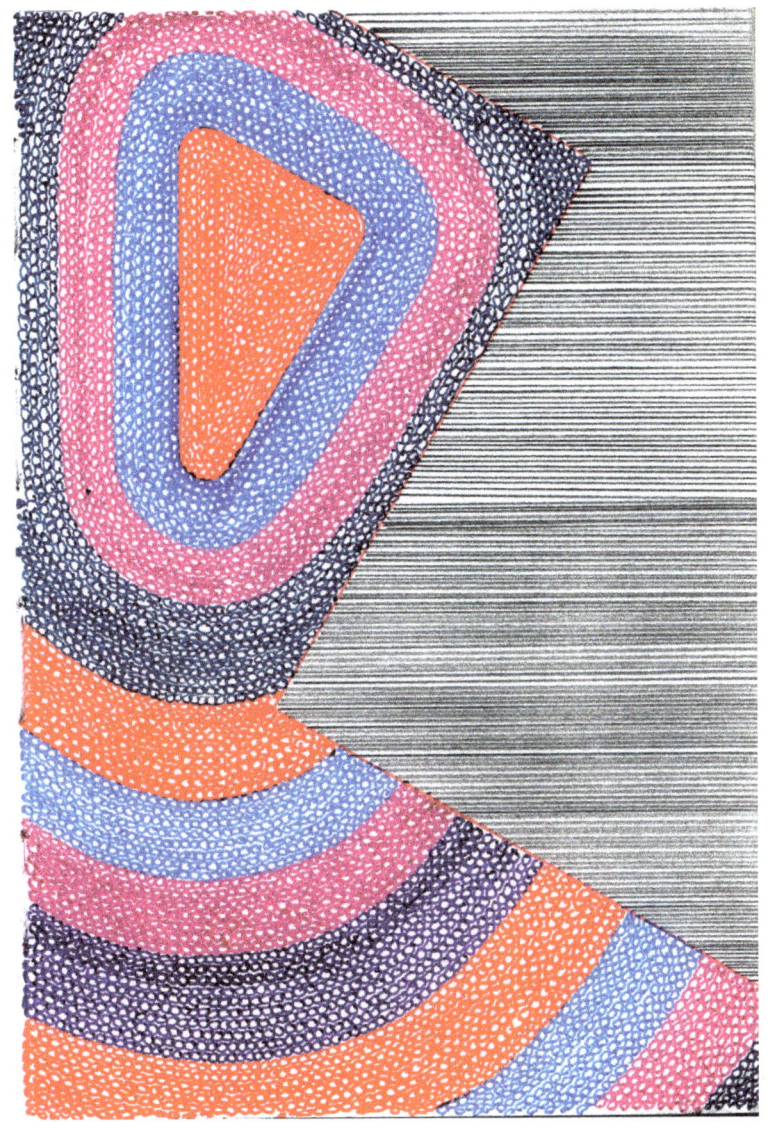

Chain-link migration

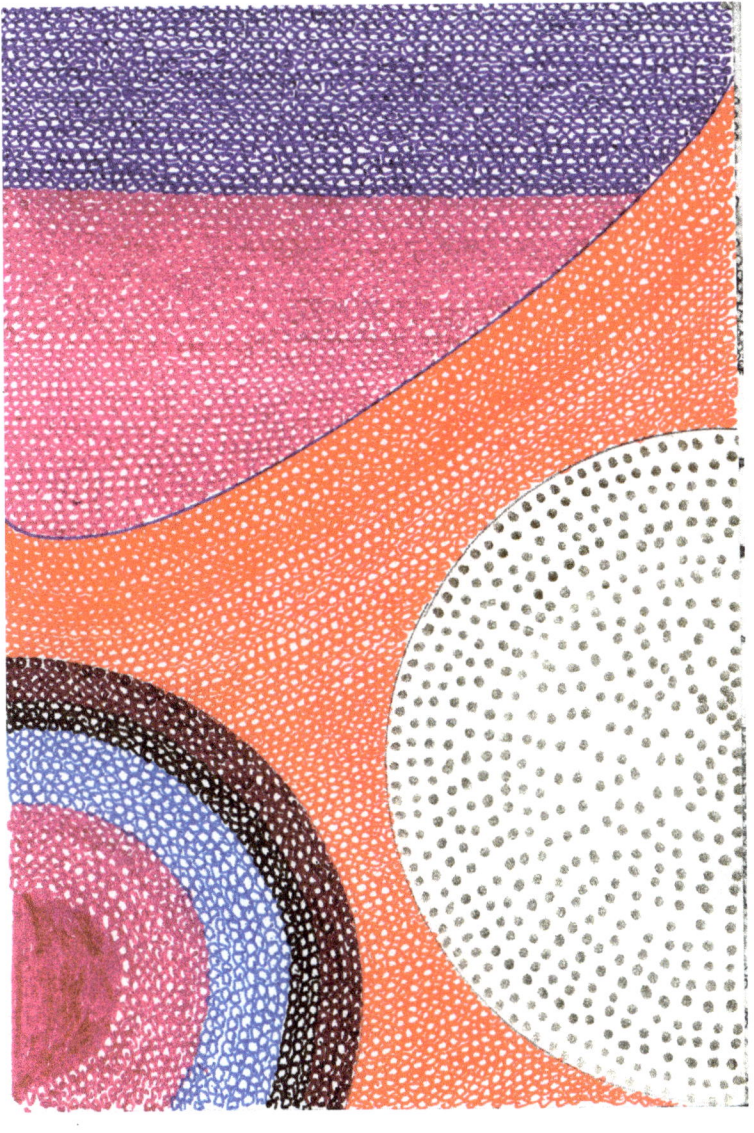

Intermittent genocide

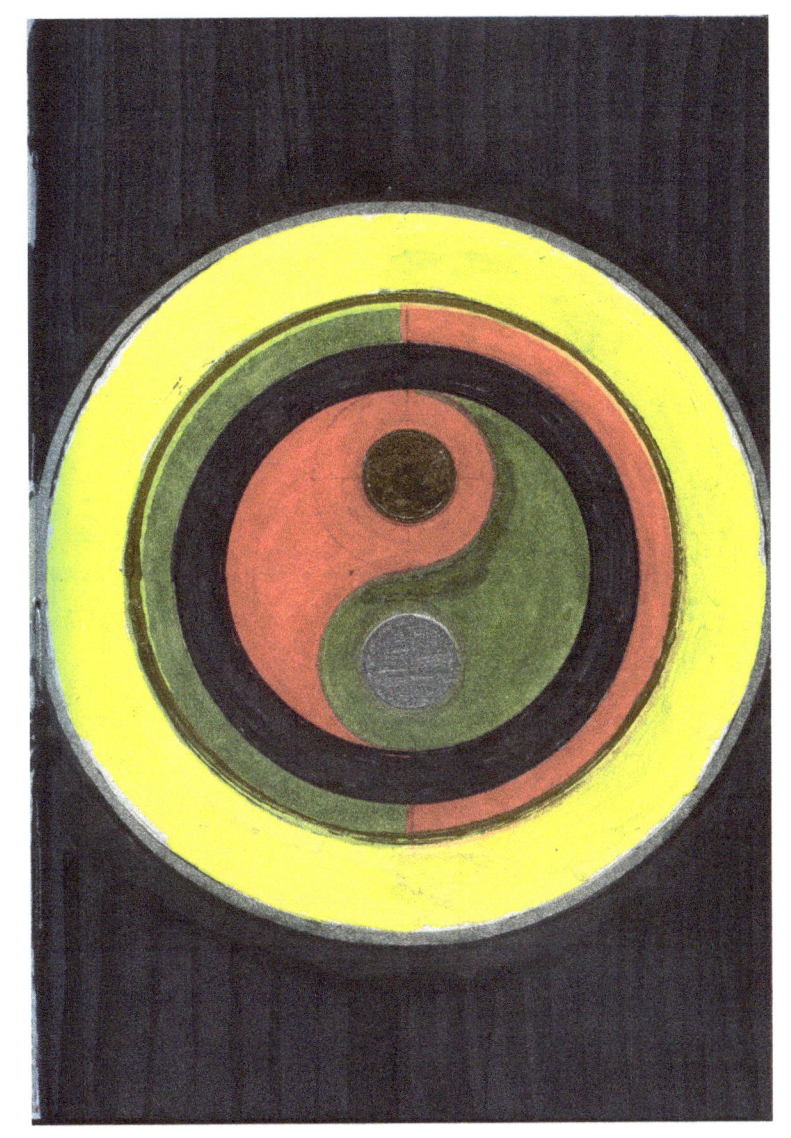

A
seat
at the
table
in a
safe house

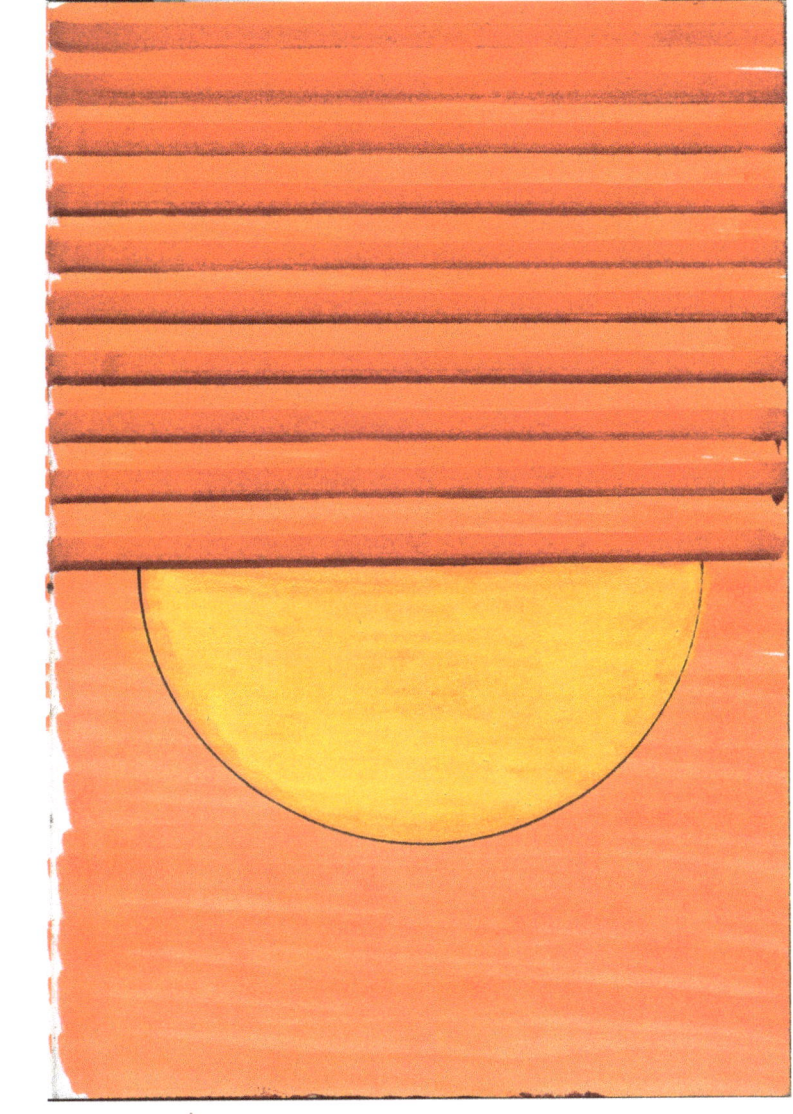

Collapsing echo-system

Turing testicles

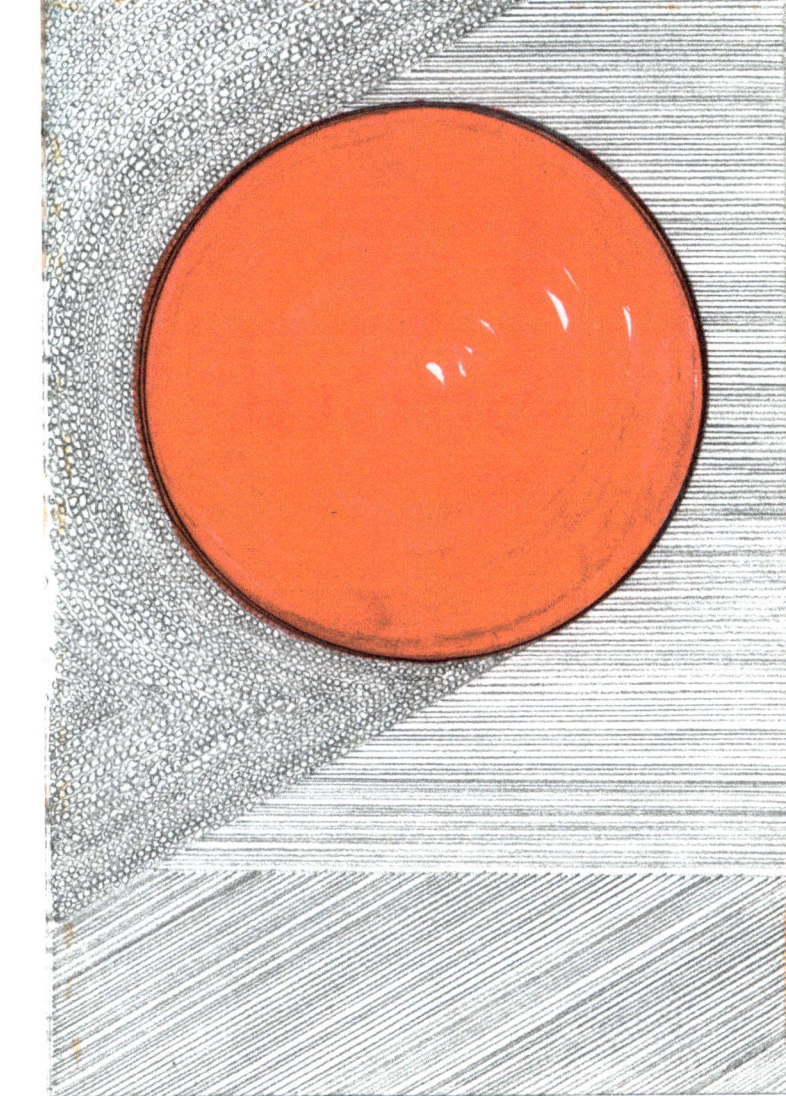

Prosecutors will be violated

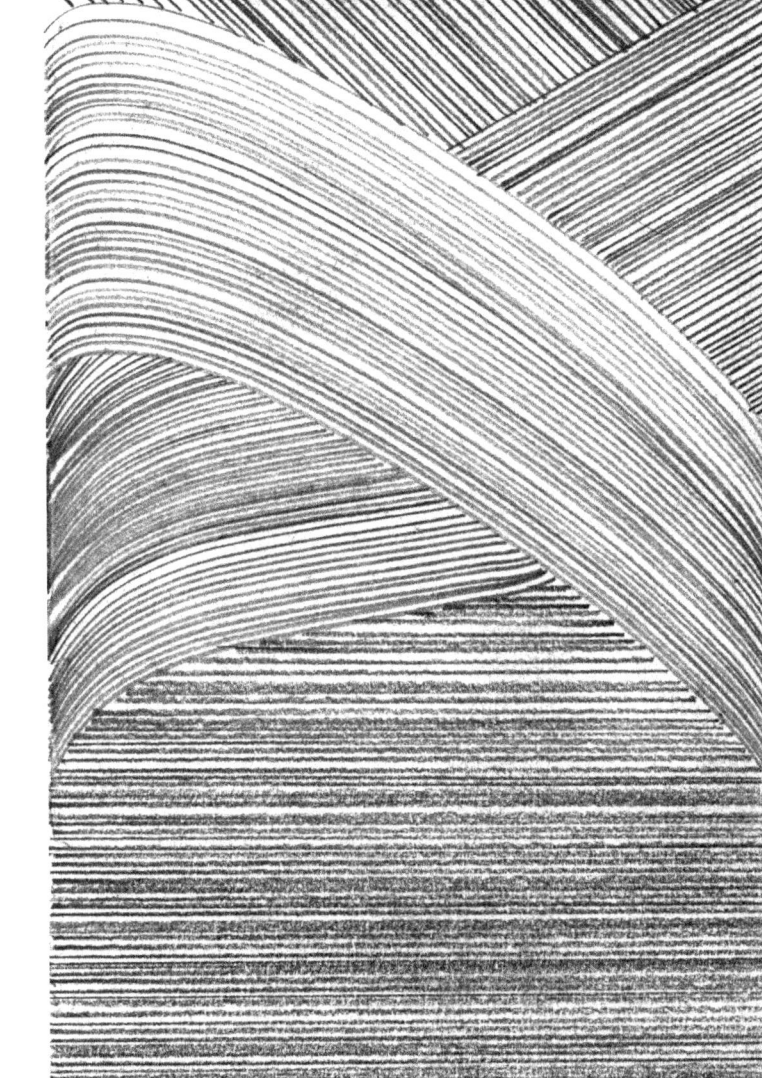

I have known Victor for more than 30 years, and loved his art for almost that long (it took him awhile before he would show it to me). When he said that he would let his art accompany my words, I was happy and flattered. To select the words that appear in this book, I chose the number of phrases to match the number of pages in the book. I printed the phrases and cut them into individual strips. I placed the strips in a bag and then pulled them out with the first one going on the first page, the second on the second page, and so on. I did not know what images Victor would choose for any given block of text.

Thank you: everyone at Bamboo Dart Press who helped get this book done, Kelli B, Sam Beam, and Jon Langford.

- Robert Vodicka

Although I've always appreciated abstract art it never occurred to me to make any. I started making abstract pieces in small sketchbooks in 2017. My father suffered a stroke and I was always with him in hospitals and board and cares. When my dad would be in hospitals he didn't want to small talk or watch tv or read or anything. He'd put a towel over his face and just wait. So I bought a 4" x 6" sketchbook that I could take anywhere like doctor appointments or pharmacies. At first I didn't know what to draw. I started doodling nonesense. But then one day inspired by Nick Blinko's art I started to draw small circles. The first time I filled a page it was very fullfilling. They were meditations. I would just start drawing and fill the page as ideas came to me. It was very freeing and relaxing.

Thank you Dennis Callaci and the Bamboo Dart Press family.

- Victor Gastelum

had sent me a list of words—something he had been doing—and said that if I found any use for them to use them. I had thought of self-publishing a book of my abstract pieces, but then I thought that these could go together. I thought we were doing something similar on our own in our free time. He had done a lot of writing for music ad copy and liner notes, as well as being a writer by profession; a real technical writer. I am a graphic artist. I do commercial art as well. This utilized both skills we have, but in an abstract way. I saw that they went together. I didn't understand it at first, but then we came up with a format of how to put the two together.

DC: In initial conversations, one of you mentioned that the book was going to consist of fake band names ascribed to each of Victor's works. It could still be read as such, but it's become something larger than that in my eyes.

Robert Vodicka: At some point I was making up band names to entertain myself. I was putting words together that I thought were interesting juxtapositions; interesting word play. I think it started with band names. I'm not sure if that started first, or if they were two parallel vectors, but it expanded into me writing things down that occurred to me. Prior to the pandemic, I was driving around Illinois for work quite a bit, so to entertain myself on long boring

Dennis Callaci (Bamboo Dart Press, Refrigerator, Shrimper Records and Tapes) interviewed Victor Gastelum and Robert Vodicka over Zoom on November 7, 2021. The interview was edited for clarity.

Dennis Callaci: The subtext of how and why these pieces were created adds an emotional punch. Victor, this is a new form for you. I recall you mentioning when your father was hospitalized that you bought some pens and a notebook to have something to do as you bedsat. That you couldn't focus on reading or anything else.

Victor Gastelum: Yeah, I had a notebook at hand on a visit and I started drawing small circles, as small as I could, until I filled up the page. At first I tried to draw things, like Nick Blinko does; crucifixes and things in the little circles, but I couldn't. I couldn't even imagine how he [Blinko] does what he does, so then I just started drawing abstractly. I liked it. I got into it. I filled up a couple of sketchbooks and I liked that I could do it anywhere. I looked forward to waiting in line at the pharmacy. I was like, "Oh, fifteen minutes; I'm going to go sit and draw for fifteen minutes." I drew while waiting for appointments; while waiting for the doctors to come in. Any time I had to wait, it was something fun I could do. I had been doing these drawings and maybe I shared them with Robert. He

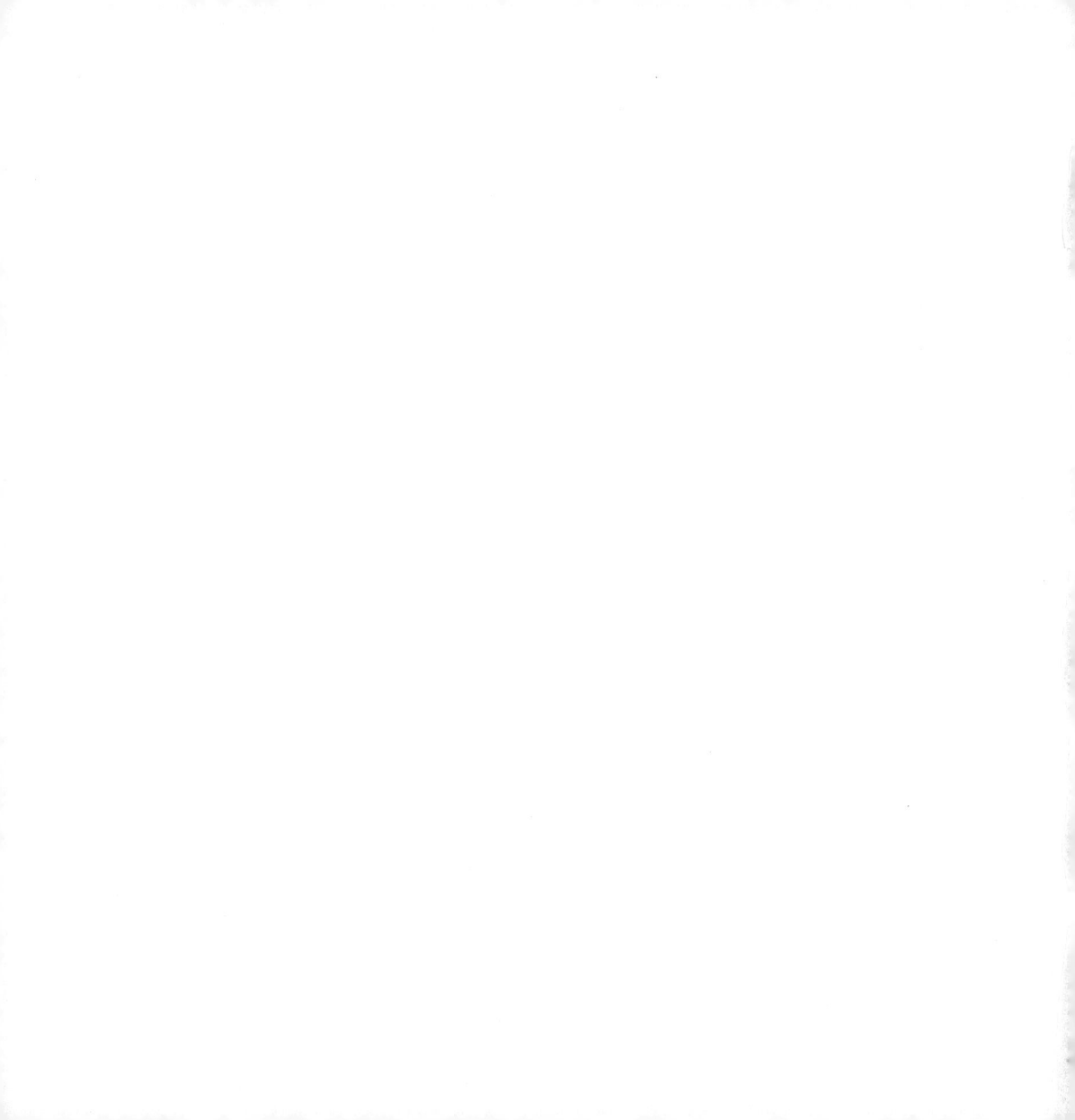

An interview with
Victor Gastelum and Robert Vodicka
conducted by Dennis Callaci

drives, I would think of these things and when I got where I was going, I would try to write them down before I forgot them.

DC: Victor, you were talking about Nick Blinko earlier. He has mental health issues and a lot of his drawings were a way to get out what was in his mind. You were in the hospital with your dad who you couldn't communicate with at that time. What fascinates me about this book is that your dear friend of decades then put words to these works. I think of that in regard to what Robert was saying, as a writer. He came up with phrases; maybe he had a notebook to get them down or maybe they were lost to the wind. You have employed other people's language in your art before.

VG: I've done that in the past when I've done comic strips; not really traditional comic strips. I'll write down a bunch of quotes—I'll make them up or hear them from people—take them from anywhere, really. I would then take them and mix them with my images. Once I put them together, they belong together; they work together. It didn't need to make obvious sense. Putting the imagery and the text together made a narrative, so I had done that sort of thing before. I liked the idea of doing that with these images. Once Robert showed me the word lists that he had done, the two went together very naturally. We've known each other for so long that it was all really easy to do. That's always the best. When you already have a relationship with somebody and then an idea to do something creative comes along, then it's really easy. It just feels right. You're not worried about the reception of it. One of my best friends said something like, "Who's gonna buy this shit?" [laughter all around] which was easy to respond to. I told him that I didn't care about that. That's not what I ever think about with anything I've ever done. Even when people do buy my art, it's not the transfer of money that matters to me. It makes me happy that someone wanted it, that they want to live with it, that the work is going to be up in their house. That's what I like. I like for people to see it.

DC: There was always a large division between art and commerce for both of you. Neither of you came to do what you were doing creatively based on money. This work, to me, is a succinct boiling down of all your experience at New Alliance and SST; Robert being a DJ at KSPC and the two of you collaborating in a weird way on ad copy for those labels. Robert, you were instrumental in helping bands and labels from the Inland Empire and greater Los Angeles area in the 1990s. I feel all of that in this book. You perversely were going to initially use your nom de plume of Roger Mexico as a credit for this book, which

was your on-air name at KSPC. Your brief titles here bring to mind succinct record reviews at the radio station or early poetry writing you did at that time for the college newspaper.

> RV: A lot of people wrote poetry in college [laughs]. Some of my stuff was published in the five-college paper, *Collage*, at that time, sure. In terms of helping bands from the late eighties into the early nineties, I had learned a certain amount working in various parts of the music business. If there were people I knew, or friends of friends that might need some help in the studio, or with mastering or anything like that, I was happy to help. I wasn't trying to become a producer or a manger of bands or anything; I was just trying to help.

DC: Interesting that intersection as well – New Alliance and SST - where the two of you also met Joey Burns. It forms a triptych; the work the three of you did early on together under the umbrella of SST Records and what became of your work after that. Victor, I know that you cold-called SST and brought down your portfolio for them to see. Was that when Robert was there? Robert, did you precede Victor at SST?

> RV: I worked out of the SST offices but my assignment, as it were, was to run New Alliance Records. I didn't have much to do with what SST was. I was just

housed in the same building. I don't know when the transaction happened as far as when Mike Watt sold New Alliance to Chuck Dukowski, Greg Ginn, and Mugger. I was hired in March of 1988 to restart the label. Victor, did you start in 1989?

VG: Yeah, 1989.

RV: Victor did the art for the first Nothing Painted Blue album, which I also worked on in the mastering phase. That may have been the first convergence.

DC: That record features Mike Neelon on the bass; prior to his exit and Joey Burns joining the band.

VG: That was the first record that I did everything on and had total freedom. The band didn't give me much direction. I always wanted to do album covers; that's how I ended up at SST. Once I was there, I found out what the job at SST really was. It wasn't what I thought. I found out that different labels treat album art differently. There were certain labels like Blue Note, Sub Pop, Nettwerk, and 4AD that had consistent album cover art, but once I got to SST, I realized that was not the philosophy there. The art was secondary. The guys running the show thought the art was cool or whatever, but that's not what they were concerned with. They were concerned with the music, the bands, live performances, and quality control of the music.

Cover artwork was secondary. What does the band want for cover art? Do they want a photo for the cover? Can they lay out the cover art like some bands could? Some bands had no idea, and that's where I would have the chance to do a bit more design work.

Then I got to design an album cover for Nothing Painted Blue and that was cool. That was my introduction to the Inland Empire scene at the time. We were driving out for shows out there; all of these great bands and some on the Shrimper label too. I loved all of that stuff; I used to listen to the cassettes at SST all the time. I did the first Refrigerator single and was kind of surprised that you asked me to do it because you guys could do it yourself. You'd done so many releases by yourself on the label by that time; you didn't need me to do it. I got the front cover photograph from Catherine Guffey with a note that read, "You can use this if you want," and I was like, "Yeah, I am going to use it!"

DC: You both have humility and keep your thumbprints off of so much of the work that you've done. Victor, I remember some early work of yours that I first got wasn't even signed; it was just rubber stamped. The releases on New Alliance that Robert played a large part in, you would not gather that from the liner notes nor in him trying to take credit for really anything.

That kindness extends to Joey Burns, who you both worked with prior to his stint in Nothing Painted Blue, Giant Sand, or the formation of Calexico. I read somewhere that Joey had said to Victor before any of this that he was going to form a band and have all of his record covers made by you.

> VG: I couldn't believe that it ended up happening. We were having a sandwich somewhere and Joey was always so excited, just a happy friendly person, and he was excited to make music; to start a band. He liked my art and said, "I like your art and I'm going to start a band and you're going to do all the album covers." It's almost like something that you tell each other when you're both ten years old, you know? The thought is so sweet, but the reality of it is a big deal. How do you form a band? How do you record? It's a lot of work to get to that point. Looking back on it, he did it—we did it. Like I said earlier, when you already have that connection with a friend and then a project comes along, then it's really easy. The project just makes itself. We already believed in each other, and it was a lot of fun working with Joey. He would push me. I remember on one of the last records that we did together, he kept wanting more. He wanted more images. "These are great—make more." So I did. It pushed me to do more than we used. My stencils later

in our relationship got kind of complicated where there are six stencils and the size was 24x36 inches. It got out of control. He made me go back to where it was just one or two stencils. A little simpler. We would work together like that; a real collaboration.

DC: The two of you came to the music and art industry through the back door. Both of you have utilized your knowledge to not only pursue your passion in music and art, but to open the door and help others. You have charted a way to work outside of the mainstream and be successful on all fronts.

RV: Speaking to distrust of the music business, I am reminded of a line from The Mekons' song "Curse of the Mekons" that goes "call it intuition/call it luck/ but we're right in all that we distrust." [written by Mekons, Low Noise Music, BMI] I never exactly felt that way. I think that my involvement in the music business was accidental. Not entirely accidental, in that I was really interested in music and knew a certain amount about it, but when I first moved to the Los Angeles area, I was just looking for a job. I knew that I wanted to do that interview show on KSPC, *Included Middle*, from '87 and '88 where I would interview bands. I would splice the tape and my voiceovers with the music. I knew I wanted to do that, and I was just trying to find a job so that I could live in that area. I found a job at an independent distributor, which was not accidental because they gave me a test at the interview and asked, "What do you know about independent music labels?" At that point I knew a lot, so they hired me. I was there for about a year and learned a lot about the music business. As shocking as this may sound, there were some independent distributors that were a little bit sketchy in their business practices in those days [laughter]. I left, but had the thought that I had learned a lot in that year and maybe there's somewhere I can apply what I learned; a place where I actually believe more in what's going on. That's how I ended up working at New Alliance. I learned and grew while I worked there. Before that job, I had never been in a mastering studio. I learned a lot from someone else we should at least mention, John Golden. An incredible mastering engineer, from Neil Young and on and on. John did all of the iconic SST stuff, as well as a bunch of Shrimper stuff for you. I learned a ton from him, and he was incredibly generous with his time and insight. Working at New Alliance, I worked with Greg Ginn pretty closely and I learned a ton from him about the music business and about how to think about music within the wider culture and the wider economy. The job gave me access to learning more things and, as I was learning them, I was helping folks. Not just anyone, but if I knew people and I liked what they were doing and it seemed like they would be easy to work with, I would help.

DC: Between the *Included Middle* radio show and the on-air back and forth with famed KSPC DJ Bill Chen, you delved into the weeds of underground music at that time. It wasn't even the usual "left of the dial" fare; the two of you were voracious listeners that would play a spectrum of noise, pop, and free jazz and would then get into hilarious/fascinating arguments about the music you were playing. A radio show isn't that different from opening the doors to a gallery. Here's what I think is a couple hours' worth of the most interesting work out there. Victor, you didn't show your work until the latter half of the 90s, correct?

VG: Well, the first time I ever showed work was at the dA Gallery in Pomona for that *Crump Comics* show that you guys put on. That was the first time and it was so cool. I just brought a bunch of my art and I asked you, "Where do I put this up?" You saw how much it was and you pointed to a wall and said, "Right there—just fill up the wall." I just put it all up and it was so fun. I never did that again. It wasn't framed. Like Raymond Pettibon would do; it was pinned up and not signed. Soon after that, I started showing my work. The funny thing was that Robert was my biggest cheerleader, and then he left. I don't think you went to any of my shows.

RV: [laughs] Well, yeah, I left New Alliance and then I left the country!

VG: He would tell me, "You are going to be showing in museums; you are going to be showing in galleries." And I just kind of doubted it. I couldn't see how that happened. I liked the art in galleries and museums, but I couldn't see myself getting there. I'd go to a gallery and look at the price sheet and the bio and it was always "MFA" [Master of Fine Arts]. Always. Back then, there were definite rules. You are not going anywhere. Without an MFA, you will be in the outsider art category. Like in *Animal House* when the nerds go to the ritzy frat house to pledge and the preppy rich guys take them to the couch where there are minorities or goofy people—I saw the art world like that. How can you even get there?

I met Raymond Pettibon coincidentally when I first started working at SST. Not at SST, because he was already gone by then, but I met him at that same time and we became friends. He was already a legend by then. I saw what he did with his art career. He didn't have an art degree. He didn't go to art school at all. He had an economics degree. The other thing was that he didn't paint. Back then, illustration and prints were not "art." If you wanted to be a visual artist, you had to be an oil painter. If you wanted to hang with the big boys. They made him do some oil paintings for one of his first big shows. They bought him canvases and he just kind of painted what he drew, and they didn't sell. He was like, "Fuck this. I'm not going to be buying canvases and oil paints—those materials are expensive." He kept doing what he was doing: drawings, no frames, just pinning them up. That was also unacceptable. Not even in art school would you see that. When you presented your art, it needed to be framed. Not Raymond; he pinned them up and he would have a hand-done price list that just had the prices by the size: 11x14 for 20 dollars; 8.5x11 for 15 dollars; or whatever. For a long time, that's how he did it. He would make his own comic books and sell them at places or give them away. The majority were just given away. He just kept going and going. I asked him once if he ever doubted his success—that he would be successful—and he said, "No. I knew that I couldn't be ignored forever." He inspired me to think that it was possible—that you could end up in a gallery. He showed me the art world, as he was already in there.

It was kind of like that with the music industry as well. I'm thinking it's one thing and it's not that at all. They say there are no rules in art, but the minute you get to the art world, there are nothing but rules. I got to see that it wasn't what I thought it was. I still participated in it; I showed my art for a long time. It was always so hard. It was so much work. I started showing less and less. I'm still doing things now. I still make the occasional record cover; flyers once in a while. Now that my kids are grown, I'm thinking I can start doing something again. What that is, I don't know. Just like with the stencils, I didn't know. When I first started going to art galleries, I would see this art and I would say, "How do you get your art here?" I looked at the art I was doing that was more like RapidographTM—real intricate drawings—and I thought, "Well, it ain't going to be this stuff. Real punk looking drawings; it ain't going to be this stuff that will end up there." I ended up making stencils and that ended up being my primary medium. Now it's the same with the abstract pieces. I like them. Even when I did the stencils then, a lot of my friends were really bummed. They wanted me to keep drawing the kind of things like when I was doing punk flyers.

DC: To be an artist and not be tethered to the past, to do new things, is the mark of someone that not only has vision but also the wherewithal to not be concerned about losing your audience. Something incredible about this book is that this is the first time the two of you have worked

together outside of some exterior business component.

RV: It's the first time that something we have worked on together is appearing under our own names. We worked on a ton of stuff together when I was at New Alliance, like ads for fanzines and magazines. Less so the album art, because the album art was more what the band or artist wanted. Victor and I would sometimes have some tension around this...

VG: I think you used to say, "It's not about what you want."

RV: [laughing] I did! I would tell you that all the time. He would try to put some of his own stuff in there and I would tell him it's what the band wants, not what he wants. There are things, particularly the New Alliance ads, that bear the marks of both of our aesthetic sensibilities, but that's not something we had under our names. This is the first project that is ours and not under the auspices of another band or record label. I didn't know what you were going to do for this project, Victor. I'd been doing these word things for my own entertainment, but if they had never come out, it wouldn't have mattered to me. At some point I got the idea that you could look at them. I think we were talking on the phone and I described to you what I was doing and sent them to you. I was flattered that you wanted to take this weird little thing I was doing and put it next to your art. I thought, "This is really going to debase Victor's art!"

VG: I knew before I even saw it that I was going to like it and want to use it. I already knew. We were already friends and really close, so it was a sure thing. Especially if we're not thinking about how are we going to market this; not worrying, "Who's going to buy it?"

RV: Whatever images you wanted to put into the book would have been fine with me, but I do like it now that you've chosen this vector of your art rather than, to the extent that you are known, your stencil art. I love all of those. The last time you visited me, we had one of the old pieces you had given me thirty years ago framed. I love all of that work. I think it's interesting and I also like for this project that it's not that; that it's a different vector of your art that's going to be next to my text.

VG: It makes more sense. It could have worked the other way too, I suppose, but to me, these make more sense. The idea that you had thought of them as band names or song titles; I think you and I love music so much that it's always in there. I thought about that with my abstract pieces too. They reminded me of psychedelic bands: Spacemen 3, Loop…repetitive things like that. I can't help it; I always make that connection to music. Sometimes I would spray paint a stencil then I would lift it and I would spray paint some silver or gold so it would just splash, and I remember telling Joey that that was feedback. It is kind of like... there's no control. There is control in that I know I lift it and I spray it—that something is going to happen—but what happens, I can never do again. I love feedback. I like guitar players. I like when the guitar player is wailing abstractly.

DC: As you worked on these drawings, you didn't have to cut, stop, etc.; you just dropped the pen and we can see where you moved. With some of them, however, you can see that there is forethought behind it because the pattern that intersects is slowly built to allow for space or repetition. They do echo back to some of your stencil work.

VG: Yeah, yeah... a little later, I went towards that. I always do that. I start with something that's easy and simple and then it evolves to where it's a job; where it's too much work. Along the way it's fun. I started using tools. I started drawing yin yangs and making up my own yin yangs. I like the idea of yin yangs. The size of the little sketchbook is four by six inches, so it's small. The size of the book dictates what happens. I might start drawing something but then I can't have my hand there anymore, so then something different has to happen. Sometimes my pencils were not sharp and I would be somewhere and I would just get as much as I could out of the pencil and blacken the whole page in. I did that a few times. Sometimes I would write on top of it afterwards. Sometimes I would just leave the page black and that was just as satisfying. The fact that I didn't have sharp pencils to start drawing something made me do that instead: fill up the page. I was using colors too. I started buying markers and grease pens. It has been real fun to experiment and maybe that will lead to something else. Maybe it will give me another idea, or I will incorporate it into other stuff I've done.

DC: I will share that, after seeing the two of you work on this book for a few years, I was struck by the caretaking you did for each other. This is a book about Victor taking care of his parents, of Robert taking care of Victor, and vice versa. Considering one another. It's there on the page.

VG: You raise your kids and then you think you're done, but then your parents need help. My parents are in their 80s. My dad just turned 90, so you're just busy as a family person with that. Today, I'll go over there to be with my dad and I'll shave and shower him and stuff. I'll have lunch with him and bring my sketch books; sit around and watch some TV. During the commercials, I'll start doing a drawing.

DC: This discussion following the art and poetry of the book is done out of having respect for the viewer; the reader. They can bring what they have to it and, should they want to read the background, they are here with us now. Without being too pretentious, I love the loss of words—the divide of the page between the script and the drawing. The whole of it together speaks of a deep friendship and a creative spring; doing something that is new for each of you that echoes all of the work that you have done prior to now. The book does not need this interview. It does not need explaining. It is a profoundly moving marriage on its own.

VG: It took a long time to put it together, but it was all there. My life has been pretty busy and it's hard to find time. I always have a circus going on.

RV: I would send something to Victor and he would sit with it, and then he would send something back to me and I would sit with it. Sometimes I had to think about it on my side and then sometimes, as with Victor, I was just very busy. "When can I find a dedicated time to get back to this?" So there is a little bit of analogy to the kind of digital recording that people do now where you send "tracks" to people and not be in the same room to make the record together. I don't know if that sounds like too much of a stretch, but hearing the two of you talk just now, there seems to be a rough analogy there.

VG: Yeah, there is always that analogy between visual art and music because they are both art. Maybe technically it's different, but creatively it's real similar. Years ago, my sister said to me, "All of your friends are musicians, writers, and artists." I thought, "Yeah, they are."

RV: You just noticed that? [laughing]

VG: I just thought, "What else would they be?" That's what I do. Music is the big connection between them. People have often asked me if I play an instrument and I say no. After they see how obsessed I am with music, they assume that I must be a musician or that I have been one. I never have—never even thought of that—but it has been a huge part of my life. It has definitely directed my life.

RV: If somebody asked Dennis that same question: "Do you play an instrument?" I think, honestly, he has to give the same answer.

DC: That's right! [laughter]

RV: It's that whole punk rock thing of you do not have to be—what's-his-name? Al Di Meola or something like that—on guitar to make music that can move people and be musical.

DC: *Elegant Gypsy* by Al Di Meola moves me every time I have to take a crap.

RV: If people like Al Di Meola, that's great; that's fine.

DC: They can fuck off!

RV: I just meant the whole punk rock thing that has distant roots in folk music. You don't have to be a virtuoso to create music or art that moves people.

DC: You're both talking about music and the process of recording music in relation to this book. Robert, it's interesting that you are discussing sending music files back and forth as many musicians do these days as similar to what the two of you did. Recently, a friend sent me some music that was recorded using this method and I was stunned. I could hear a semblance of a room and the bass did not sound like it was phoned in; the band didn't sound tethered to some steel trap that was written in stone. It worked. It works with this book, as well. It does not suffer from the methods by which it came together. It has a thread of a free jazz Rashied Ali beat; where in the hell is this going? What am I looking at? What is this?

RV: I would be very happy if people got something like that out of the book.

VG: We made it because we wanted to make it. It's like everything else I've done. This is what I'm doing right now and then that will lead to something else. I was real surprised that I started doing this. I always liked abstract art, but I've never done anything like this. I started to enjoy abstract art in the last few years, but it still didn't occur to me that that was what I was going to do. When I started doing it, it was not that I was inspired by Pollock or something. Nick Blinko's art is not abstract. There's always something going on. The texture of what he does is what I thought I could do. The limitations of where I was doing it made these pieces the way they are. I am happy with it. I would like to do bigger things. Maybe that will come from this.

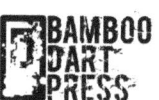

112 N. Harvard Ave. #65
Claremont, CA 91711

chapbooks@bamboodartpress.com

www.bamboodartpress.com

www.ingramcontent.com/pod-product-compliance
Lightning Source LLC
Chambersburg PA
CBHW040128230526
45473CB00032B/3047